GORE.

A...

SUE LOVERIDGE

TEACHER
TIMESAVERS

Published by Scholastic Publications Ltd,
Villiers House,
Clarendon Avenue,
Leamington Spa,
Warwickshire CV32 5PR

© **1993 Scholastic Publications Ltd**

Author Sue Loveridge
Editor Magdalena Hernas
Sub editor Noel Pritchard
Series designer Joy White
Design co-ordinator Lynne Joesbury
Design and illustration Oxford Illustrators
Cover illustration Frances Lloyd
Cover photograph Martyn Chillmaid

Processed by Pages Bureau, Leamington Spa
and Oxprint, Oxford
Printed in Great Britain by Clays Ltd, Bungay, Suffolk

British Library Cataloguing-in-Publication Data
A catalogue record for this book is
available from the British Library.

ISBN 0-590-53122-0

Contents

This book is designed to save teachers valuable time and provide a ready source of illustrative material for use in the classroom. The illustrations cover a broad range of curriculum areas and include topics such as: transport; living things; dinosaurs; musical instruments; sports; everyday objects; water; weather; the solar system; history; native art and road safety.

The illustrations may be photocopied for immediate use or traced for overhead projection purposes to suit the needs of the teacher. There are no accompanying labels on the photocopiable sheets but for identification purposes the less obvious illustrations will be named in the list below.

Transport

Page 9 is on the subject of space travel. The illustrations include: a rocket and a space shuttle, a vehicle which marked a new era of space travel, as it can return to Earth from space and be used again, whereas earlier craft were not sophisticated enough to do this and had to be rebuilt; a lunar module, the part of the space craft that actually lands upon the moon or planet surface; Skylab, a space station, and an astronaut's space suit, without which humans would not survive the harsh conditions of space.

Pages 10 – 12 show stages in the early development of air transport. On page 10 there is a Montgolfier hot air balloon and planes that were used by Bleriot, the first man to fly the English Channel (top right) and the Wright brothers, the first men to build and fly a plane (bottom right). Page 11 features later models of aircraft: a Sopwith Camel; an airship; a Spitfire and a helicopter, while page 12 shows modern-day aircraft: Concorde; a microlight and Trident and jumbo jet passenger airliners.

Pages 13 and 14 depict various aspects of water transport. On page 13 are: a steam paddleboat, which was built for use on calm inland waters, most usually on the large rivers in North America; a galleon, used in medieval times for sea travel; a clipper, a nineteenth century cargo vessel and a yacht. Which of these have children seen on visits to the seaside? Page 14 features: a modern-day tanker; an ocean liner; a submarine and a hovercraft.

Page 15 is on the theme of trains. Stephenson's Rocket, one of the first steam-powered railway engines, is shown on the left; a Pacific steam locomotive, common during the 1930s, top right, and a French Mistral electric train bottom right.

Page 16 traces the history of the bicycle, from the hobby-horse style, on which there were no pedals and the boneshaker, on which the pedals were at the front, to the small-wheeled city bike of the 1970s and racing or mountain bikes of today.

Pages 17 and 18 show how cars have changed over the years. On page 17 you can see an 1888 Benz, the first motor car to be brought to England; a Ford Fiesta; a 1930s Opel-Blitz truck; a long distance juggernaut, as seen on the roads in North America and a Morris Minor from the 1950s. Have the children seen any of these cars on the road or in films and photographs? Page 18 compares racing vehicles from the past with those of today. Featured is a Zenith motorbike, a modern racing bike, a Bugatti 35 and a Formula One racing car.

The human body

Page 19 is an illustration of the human skeleton. People come in many different shapes and sizes but all have the same framework of bones. Can the children name any of the bones? Can they make a moving skeleton with hinged joints?

Page 20 shows the human digestive and respiratory systems. Eating and breathing are vital bodily functions and these drawings can be used to explain the processes involved. Do all animals have the same digestive and respiratory systems?

Page 21 features illustrations of the heart and ear. The heart pumps blood to all parts of the body. Do the children know the names of the blood vessels that carry blood? The mechanism within our ears enables us to hear. Which are the parts that respond to sound? What other functions are controlled by our ears?

Page 22 shows the human eye. Can the children identify any of the parts of the eye? The lens enables us to focus on objects at various distances. You could investigate the properties of lenses using a telescope or magnifying glass.

Living things

Page 23 shows a variety of common household pets. To which animal families do the pets belong? Which animals are kept in cages of one sort or another? How do pets differ from wild animals? Were they wild once?

Pages 24 – 26 feature farm animals and their young that are likely to be seen on a visit to the countryside. Which of the animals are used for food? Which animals produce dairy products?

Pages 27 and 28 are on the subject of endangered species from around the world. On page 27 you can see a black rhino (Africa), an Asian elephant, a lemur (Madagascar), a condor (North and South America) and a gorilla (Africa), while on page 28 are a lynx (Europe, Asia and North America), a tiger (India) and a polar bear (Arctic).

Pages 29 and 30 show British minibeasts, including insects such as bees, wasps, ants and butterflies through to spiders, ladybirds, worms, centipedes and caterpillars. Can the children identify the different groups within the minibeast kingdom?

Page 31 depicts British wild animals. The children may have seen hedgehogs or frogs in their garden but badgers are much more rarely seen. Which animals can only be seen at night? Which animals make their homes underground? Where else do animals make their homes?

Pages 32 and 33 give a selection of British birds. Can the children identify the birds using reference books? Which ones are usually found near water? Which are birds of prey? Can you guess what sorts of food the birds eat from the shape of their beaks and claws?

Pages 34 – 36 are on the theme of sea creatures. On page 34 are: a lobster, hermit crab, jellyfish, edible crab, starfish, anemone, prawn and octopus. Some of these have claws or tentacles which they use to feed and move around. Which have the children seen before? On page 35 are a dolphin, hammerhead and white sharks, a manta ray and a turtle, all of which are more likely to be seen in a zoo aquarium than at the local seaside resort. Page 36 illustrates a sea horse, salmon, eel, plaice, tunny fish and a mackerel. What is the actual size of these creatures? Which fish is the biggest and which the smallest? Have the children seen any of the animals in shops or on visits to the seaside?

Pages 37 and 38 show trees, with accompanying drawings of the flowers, seeds and leaves to help in practical work and field studies. On page 37 are an elder, silver birch, hawthorn and ash, while sycamore, horse chestnut, holly and oak can be seen on page 38. Which of these are deciduous? The children could colour the leaves, flowers and seeds correctly from reference books or living examples.

Pages 39 and 40 represent the life-cycles of the frog, dragonfly, butterfly and house fly. Can the children identify the stages of development? Which animals live part of their lives underwater but when they mature are able to live on land? What is the transformation in their appearance called?

Dinosaurs

Pages 41 and 42 illustrate various dinosaurs that children will be able to find in books or natural history museums. On page 41, clockwise from top left, are: Parasaurolophus, Stegosaurus, Hylaeosaurus, Styracosaurus and Tyrannosaurus and on page 42 Ankylosaurus, Pteranodon, Brachiosaurus and Triceratops. How many years ago did dinosaurs walk the Earth? The only evidence we have left of these creatures are fossil skeletons and primitive animals that have survived the centuries, having evolved very little since they first came into existence. The pictures we see of dinosaurs today are artists' impressions based on scientific guesswork. In what ways can the children identify the environments in which these creatures used to live, and the food they used to eat, from the shapes of their bodies?

Animal features

Page 43 illustrates similarities and differences in the hands or claws of various animals. The examples shown are of a human, lobster, bird, monkey and elephant. Can you see how they are suited to their purpose? Which animals do not have hands? How do they cope?

Page 44 shows a variety of animal feet, including the frog, deer, human, lynx and duck. All of these are different in shape and form, each one suited to the animal's way of life. Which ones are from animals that live in or near water? How can you tell? Which is the claw of a carnivore?

Pages 45 and 46 feature animal faces. An elephant, a gorilla, a rhinoceros and a dog can be seen on page 45 while on page 46 are a bear, a rabbit, a donkey and a human. Children can look at the various characteristics of each animal face and say how they are suited to the animal's way of life.

Musical instruments

Pages 47 and 48 show a selection of musical instruments belonging to the woodwind family. On page 47 are a recorder, flute, clarinet, oboe, bassoon and saxophone, while on page 48 there are a trumpet, cornet, trombone, French horn, tenor horn and tuba. What do all these instruments have in common?

Page 49 features string instruments: a violin, viola, cello, double bass, acoustic and electric guitar.

Page 50 shows a range of percussion instruments, including a bass drum, kettle drum, side drum, tambourine, cymbals, triangle, castanets, cabaca and maracas.

Sport

Pages 51 – 53 feature a range of sporting activities, both individual and team sports, that the children are likely to recognise. The illustrations can be used as discussion points or to supplement ongoing projects as well as an aid for presenting sports notices, fixture lists and reports.

Everyday objects

Pages 54 – 65 are on the theme of objects that we use or see in our day-to-day lives. Page 54 illustrates a selection of toys and objects that children should be able to recognise. Have toys and games changed over the years? Do children today play the same games that their parents used to play when they were young?

Pages 55 – 60 show household objects, ranging from furniture to gardening tools and pages 61 – 65 show a variety of foods that we eat, from dairy products to vegetables.

Water

Page 66 provides a range of decorative borders and lettering that could be used to brighten up your 'Water' project.

Page 67 depicts objects associated with the seaside and could be used to help the children create their own beach scene. Are the beaches and coastline in other countries around the world similar to those in England?

Page 68 shows three artefacts that would have been found on board a narrowboat: a painted water can, a teapot and a lace-edged plate which would have been used as a wall hanging. Ask the children to colour and decorate these objects. What would life have been like for the people who lived on board narrowboats?

Page 69 shows a rose illustration, one of the colourful devices used to decorate narrowboats. Traditionally, these were painted in groups. Red petalled roses had a black background with a brown centre, yellow roses had an orange background with a brown centre and white roses had a pink background with a red centre.

Page 70 shows a range of other decorative devices that were painted on narrowboats. Can the children think of any forms of decoration that are used today (on cars, boats, bicycles)?

Weather

Page 71 gives examples of different cloud formations. Clockwise from top left: cirro cumulus; stratus; strato cumulus; cumulo nimbus; cumulus and cirrus. Can the children spot the different cloud formations in the sky? Do they know how clouds are formed? Make a collection of weather sayings. Are they accurate weather predictions?

Page 72 shows a range of weather symbols that the children may have seen on forecasts on the television or in the newspapers. Can they identify them all? Use them to record/forecast the weather. Can they make up their own weather symbols?

Page 73 is a diagram of the water cycle, which can be used to explain how water can be seen in many different forms in the world around us.

The solar system

Page 74 is a diagram of the solar system, showing the nine planets that orbit the Sun. Children could label the planets from reference books.

Page 75 shows the 12 signs of the zodiac. These signs are derived from constellations of stars and were named long ago after animals and ancient gods. The children could label the star signs.

Buildings

Pages 76 – 80 show famous historical buildings and architectural styles from around the world. On page 76 are Stonehenge, an Egyptian pyramid and the Greek Parthenon. Which is the oldest and which the most recent? On page 77 is the Colosseum, the Great Wall of China and the Taj Mahal. In which countries can these buildings be found? The Great Wall of China is so big that it can be seen from the moon. Page 78 features the Eiffel Tower, Golden Gate Bridge, Tower Bridge and the Empire State Building. Page 79 gives examples of Tudor and Queen Anne style architecture and page 80 a 'romantic' Victorian house which incorporates various architectural styles alongside a suburban Victorian villa.

History

Pages 81 – 86 are on the theme of 'Ancient Egypt'. Page 81 features a range of patterns and designs that can be found on Egyptian artefacts. These can be used to decorate project work. Page 82 shows a decorative wooden coffin inside which a mummy would have been placed. Ancient Egyptians believed that the body had to be preserved so that the spirit would recognise it in the afterlife. Pages 83 and 84 represent Ancient Egyptian gods. Osiris (the god of the dead and Lord of the Underworld), Thoth (the inventor of speech and writing and recorder of deeds of men), Horus (the sun god and bringer of life) and Sekhmet (the lion-headed goddess, bringer of war) can be seen on page 83 and on page 84 are Hapi (the goddess of water and rivers), Anubis (the jackal-headed god who weighs the scales of justice

after death), Amun (the king of gods) and Seth (the brother of Osiris, god of storms and violence). On page 85 you can see the regalia of the Pharaoh: a false beard to show he was a god; a flail and a crook, the symbols of Osiris; a vulture and a cobra worn upon his headdress to symbolise power over upper and lower Egypt and a piece of jewellery called a scarab, a symbol of the sun god. The clothing that would have been worn in everyday life in Ancient Egypt can be seen on page 86.

Pages 87 – 94 are on the theme of 'Ancient Greece'. On page 87 there is a range of Greek pottery. Can the children find the names and uses of these pots in reference books? They could colour the pots then cut them out and cut them into pieces to be used as a jigsaw. Styles of Ancient Greek architecture can be seen on page 88. The Doric and Ionic styles on the left were the earliest and from them developed the more elaborate Corinthian style. Greek gods are featured on pages 89 and 90. Page 89 clockwise from top left: Ares (God of War); Zeus (King of the gods, the land and the sky); Hermes (messenger of the gods, inventor of mathematics, the alphabet and astronomy) and Hades (king of the underworld). Page 90: Poseidon (king of the sea); Aphrodite (goddess of love) and Demeter (goddess of all plants). A Hoplite or Greek foot soldier can be seen on page 91. His helmet would have been made of bronze with a horse hair crest, and his shield of wood with a leather curtain to protect his legs from arrows. Everyday Greek dress is shown on page 92. Women wore a chiton, while men wore a simple kilt or a tunic. A himation, as seen on the right, was worn by both sexes. Pages 93 and 94 feature mythological creatures: Pegasus; the Hydra; the Minotaur; Medusa and Cyclops. Children could research Greek myths.

Pages 95 – 98 are on the theme of 'The Romans'. A Roman legionary, or foot soldier, can be seen on page 95. His helmet, or cassis, would have been made from iron with brass fittings; a loricia, made from iron plates on leather, protected his chest; a cingulum (a leather belt with an apron of metal discs) protected his waist area. He also wore sandals (caligae) and carried a shield (scutum), a javelin (pilum) and an iron sword (gladius). Page 96 shows clothes that would have been

worn in everyday life. Tunics were the most popular items of clothing; women wore a full-length tunic, called a stola, and men a toga. Page 97 gives a selection of everyday objects. From left to right: amphorae, used to store wine or oil; an oil lamp; a nail file; an ear pick and a paterae (pouring jug) with strigils (used to scrape the skin). Page 98 shows four of the many Roman gods: Mars (the god of war), Juno (Jupiter's wife and the patron goddess of women), Venus (the goddess of love and beauty) and Jupiter (the king of gods).

Pages 99 – 106 are on the theme of 'Invaders and Settlers'. Page 99 shows contrasting patterns and designs taken from historical artefacts which can be used to decorate written work or to add detail to costumes. On page 100 are details from the Fuller Brooch, an example of ninth century Anglo-Saxon jewellery and on page 101 details from Anglo-Saxon manuscripts and purse lids found at the Sutton Hoo ship burial site in Suffolk. The Fuller Brooch and Sutton Hoo Purse lids can be seen in the British Museum. Pages 102 and 103 show clothing from Anglo-Saxon times. The warrior on page 102 would have worn a woollen shirt, trousers cross-gartered with leather and leather shoes. Over this would have been a tunic, short-sleeved mail coat and cloak. Page 103 shows everyday clothing from Anglo-Saxon times. Clothing would have been made from wool or linen. Pages 104 – 106 show different aspects of Viking life. On page 104 you can see a warrior. His jerkin and leggings would have been made from sheepskin and the jacket from thick leather, often covered with metal rings or scales. They carried a battleaxe as well as a sword. Helmets were often decorated with horns or wings. Typical everyday dress can be seen on page 105. Men wore woollen breeches with leather boots or shoes and a belted overtunic with a cloak. Women wore a long tunic dress with a tabard-style garment and a headscarf (white if they were married). On page 106 is a Viking longship, the type of vessel usually associated with the Viking explorers and conquerors. There were rows of oars along each side of the ship that were used to carry them over the water.

Pages 107 – 112 feature illustrations from Tudor and Stuart times. On page 107 is the Tudor Rose, an emblem commonly found on artefacts from this era, which can be enlarged or used as a decorative device. Clothing from the reign of King Henry VIII can be seen on page 108. Clothes for the nobility of Tudor times would have been richly-embroidered and made from velvet, satin and silk. Men wore short breeches and open shoes, a short velvet cloak and flat hat while women would have worn a low, square-necklined dress with tight bodice and long skirts and a gable hood. Clothing from the reign of Queen Elizabeth I can be seen on page 109. Men's doublets were often padded and had low pointed waists, hose were worn beneath breeches. Small pointed beards were fashionable. Women wore ruffs and farthingales (a frame worn round the waist to support their dress). The poor would have worn clothes made from wool and cotton. Men wore a shirt with loose breeches and a cloak while women wore simple long dresses with an apron, woollen cap and cloth stockings. Page 110 depicts the clothes of Puritans, who believed in simple worship and wore staid, dark clothing, with large white collars. Clothing from the reign of Charles I can be seen on page 111. The pikeman is a Parliamentarian. His cloth coat was tawny orange and he wore a metal helmet and armour. The musketeer is a Royalist. He is wearing a buffalo-hide sleeveless coat with a bandolier across his chest for his ammunition. Both of the above wore breeches and stockings with boots or shoes. During the reign of Charles II (page 112) men wore long waistcoats with silk stockings, wide-legged boots and lace and ribbon trimming on the clothing. Long curled wigs and moustaches were popular. Women's dresses were heavily trimmed, often cut to show the underskirts, and hair was worn in side curls or ringlets.

Page 113 shows typical Victorian clothing. Men wore a frock coat, a waistcoat, a shirt with a stiff collar and a loosely-knotted tie. Trousers were usually a lighter colour than the jacket, and footwear comprised leather lace-up shoes or ankle boots. Top hats were fashionable. Women wore the poke bonnet and crinoline (hooped petticoat) with their hair often parted at the centre or in ringlets.

Page 114 shows typical Edwardian clothing. Men wore short jackets made from flannel or tweed, which were pleated or belted at the back, and a matching waistcoat. Trousers were narrow with turn-ups and shirts had a turn-down collar, worn with a bow or tie. Hair was short and well trimmed, moustaches were fashionable. For women, large hats were popular and necklines were high, often supported with wire or bone. Hair was piled on top of the head and often padded with false hair. Parasols were common.

Page 115 shows a soldier from World War I. His jacket and breeches would have been khaki and from ankle to knee puttees were worn for support and protection. A steel helmet protected his head and a bandolier and haversack were used to carry his gear.

Page 116 features clothing from the 1920s. Lounge suits and trilby hats were popular for men. Suits were single or double-breasted and in finely-striped or plain cloth. Overcoats were commonly worn and shoes were preferred to boots. Women's fashions were seen to change after the war. Skirts were worn to knee length and hair was cut short. Cloche hats were fashionable and rayon was used to make flesh-coloured stockings. Court shoes and high-heeled shoes were also popular.

Page 117 illustrates clothes from the 1940s. During World War II material was scarce, so clothes were designed to be functional and hard-wearing. Men's jackets were shorter with few pockets and no buttons on cuffs; trousers were narrower with no turn-ups. Women's skirts were shorter and from 1940 onwards slacks became more common both at work and leisure. Shoes were practical and low-heeled.

Page 118 shows fashions from the 1950s. It was in the 1950s that man-made fibres came into common use, widening the range of materials and styles available, and young people began to have fashions of their own, such as Teddy boy style clothing.

Page 119 depicts clothes from the 1960s. During this decade, skirt lengths became the focus of fashion. Mini skirts were popular and dress and hair styles were strongly influenced by the musical scene. Trouser suits became popular for women and there was not such a large distinction between dress for men and women as there had been previously.

Page 120 is a drawing of a modern-day soldier. All over the world, soldiers' dress is similar - practical and designed to blend in with their surroundings. A helmet and protective jacket are often worn.

Native art

Pages 121 – 125 feature designs taken from American Indian artefacts. The patterns on page 121 are taken from headbands, ceramics and fabrics. Traditional colours would have been red, yellow, black and white. Page 122 shows a Great Bear design found amongst tribes of the north-west coast of America. Page 123 is a wooden mask of the Haida tribe of North America. Page 124 depicts Ehecatl, the god of winds, found on artefacts from South America and page 125 is a masked eagle dancer found amongst the peoples of Oklahoma in North America. These pages can be used as a starting-point for design, print-making, collage and creative writing activities.

Pages 126 and 127 feature examples of Chinese decorative designs which can be found on a variety of artefacts, ranging from textiles, ceramics and paintings to architecture.

Page 128 shows African masks from the Congo, which were often made from wood and used in tribal dances and ceremonies.

Page 129 shows masks from Java. These were used in traditional drama to act out scenes from Hindu mythology.

Pages 130 and 131 show a selection of Scandinavian floral designs frequently found on china, furniture and other household objects.

Graphics

Pages 132 – 141 provide a collection of capital letters, alphabets, headings, logos and decorative borders that can be used in conjunction with other sections included in this book. Page 135 is a capital letter T from an illuminated manuscript.

Road safety

Pages 142 – 144 give a selection of British road signs. Which ones do the children see on the way to school? Can they identify the meaning of each one? (A copy of the *Highway Code* may come in useful here!) What shapes are the signs?

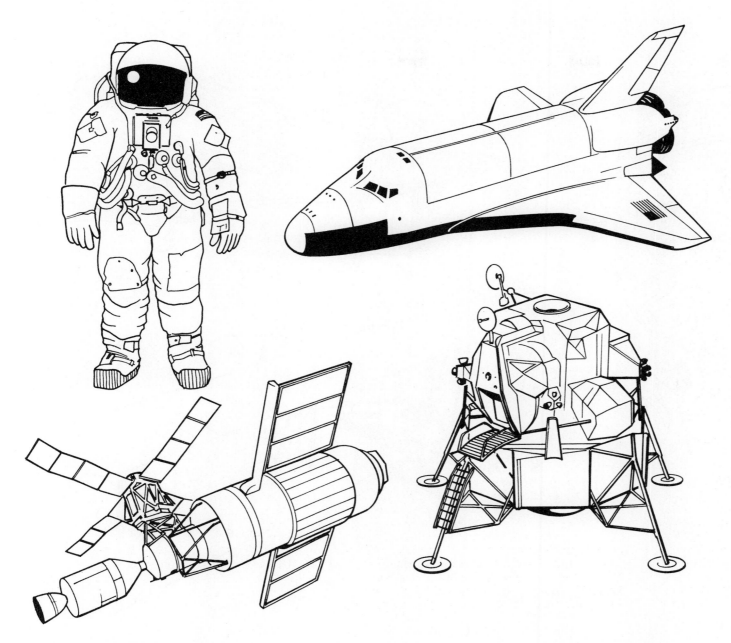
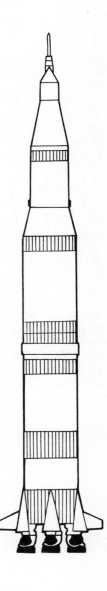

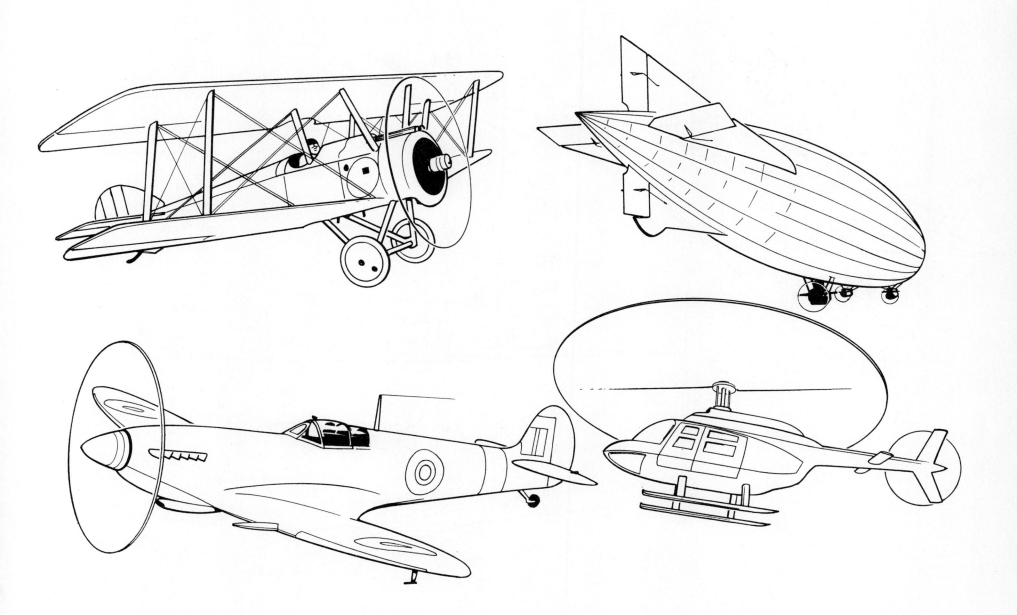

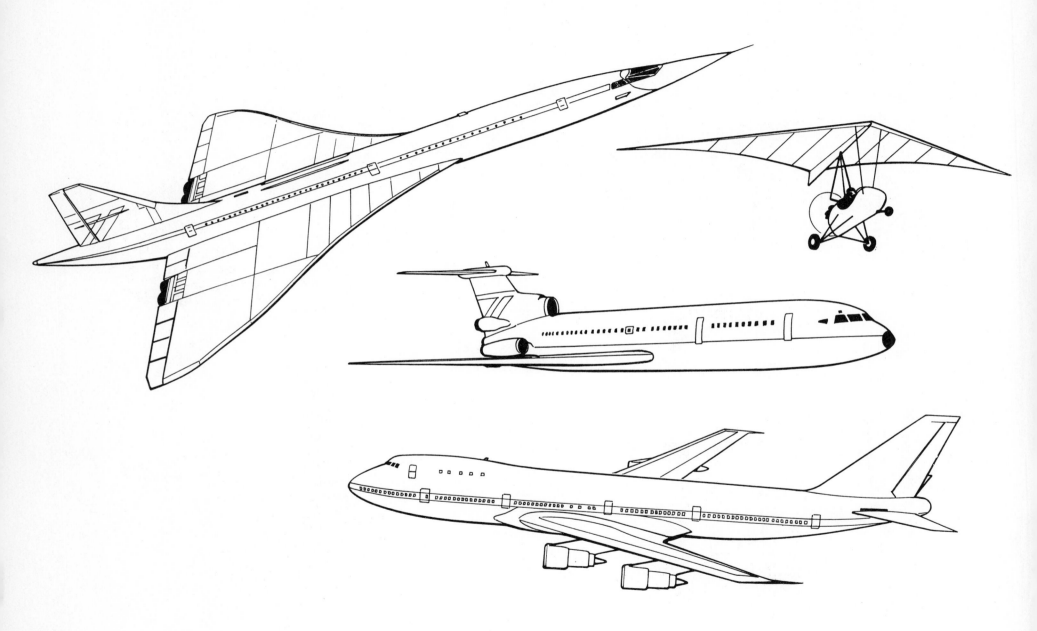

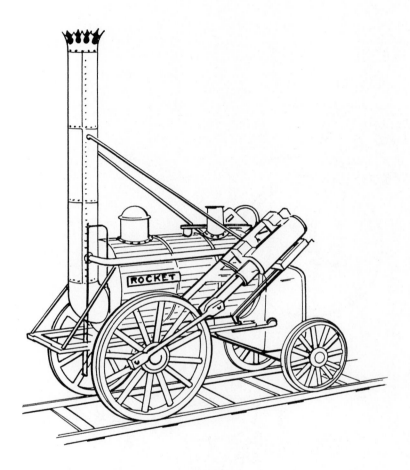

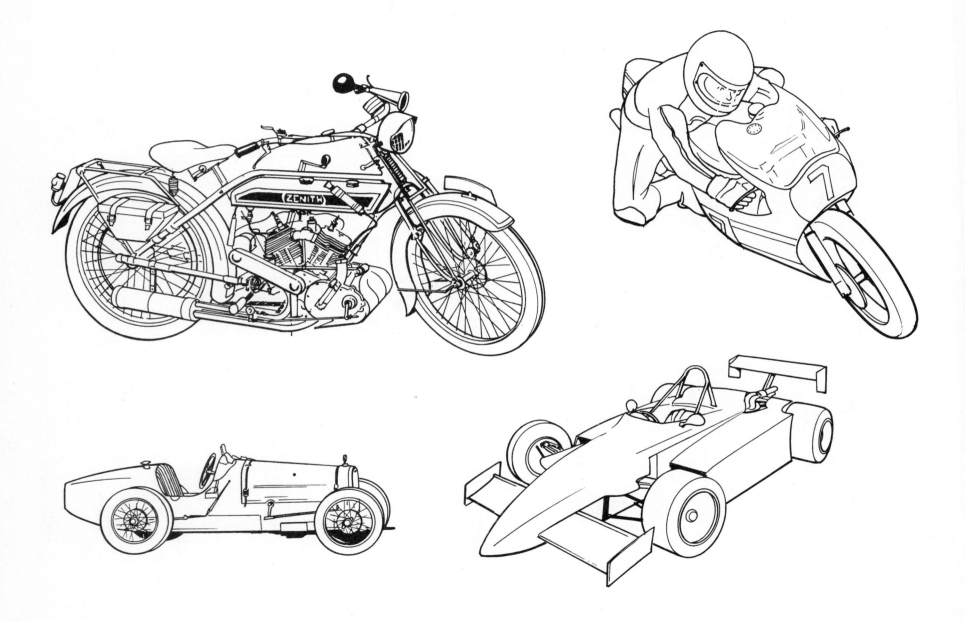

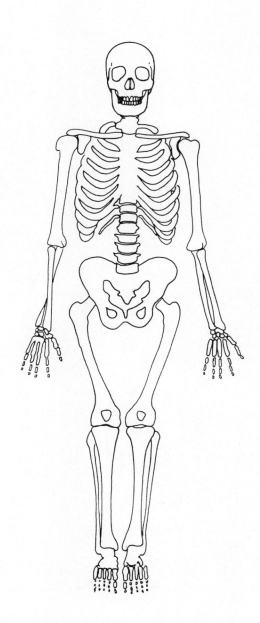
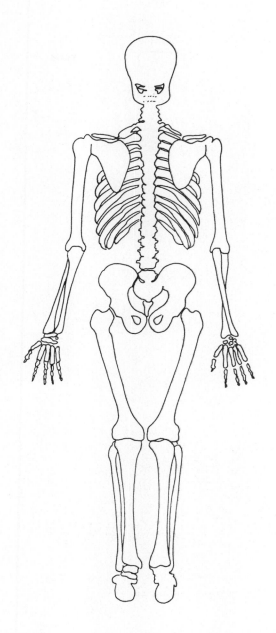

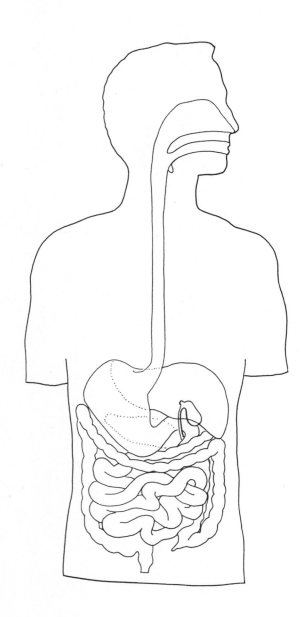

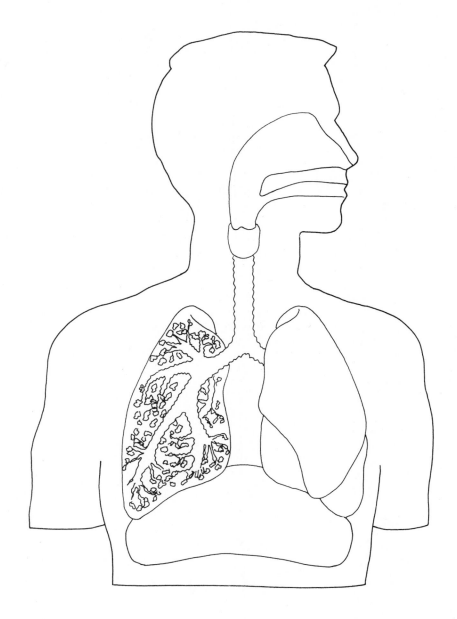

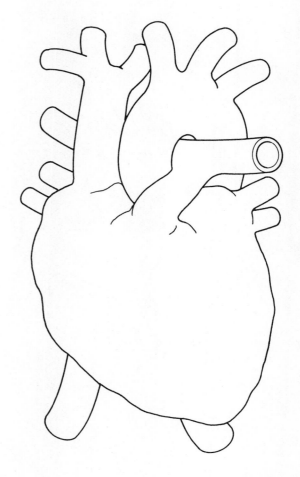

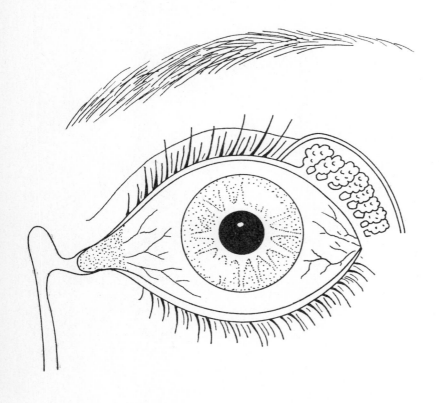

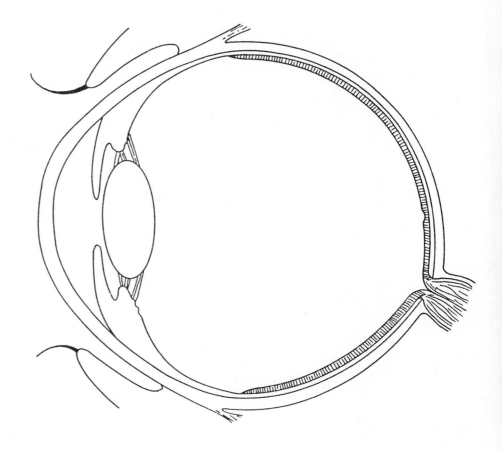

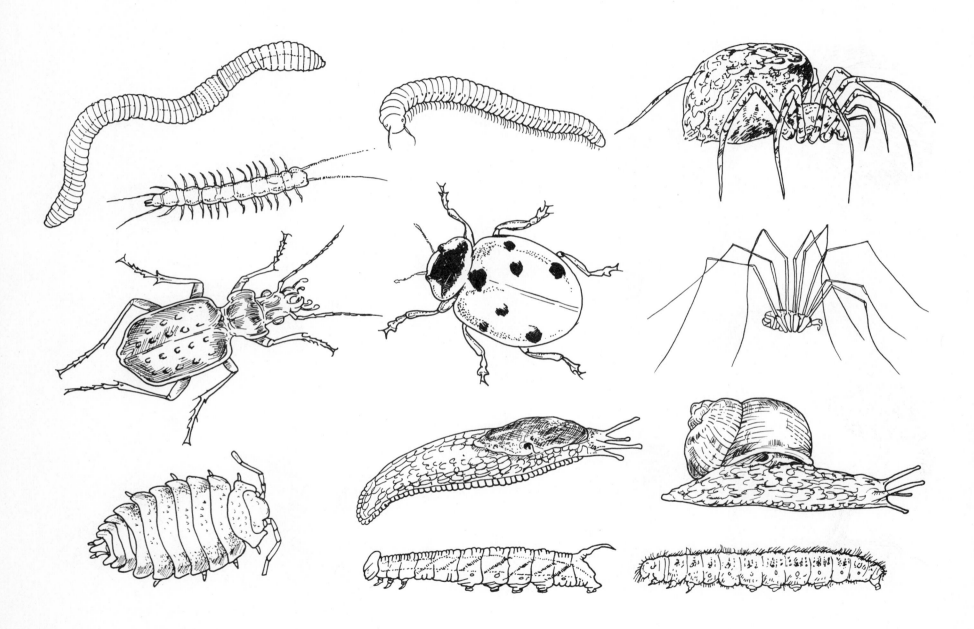

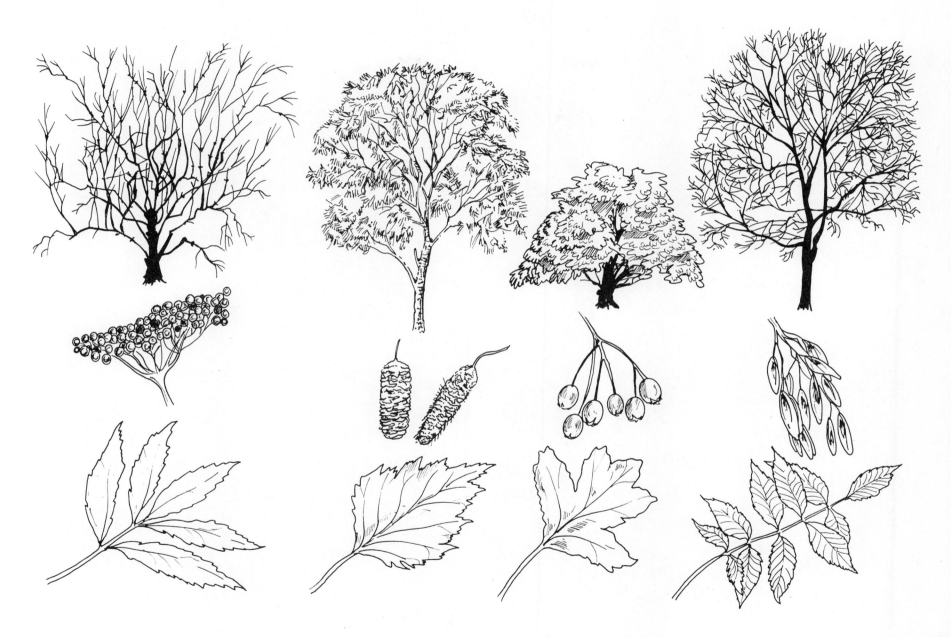

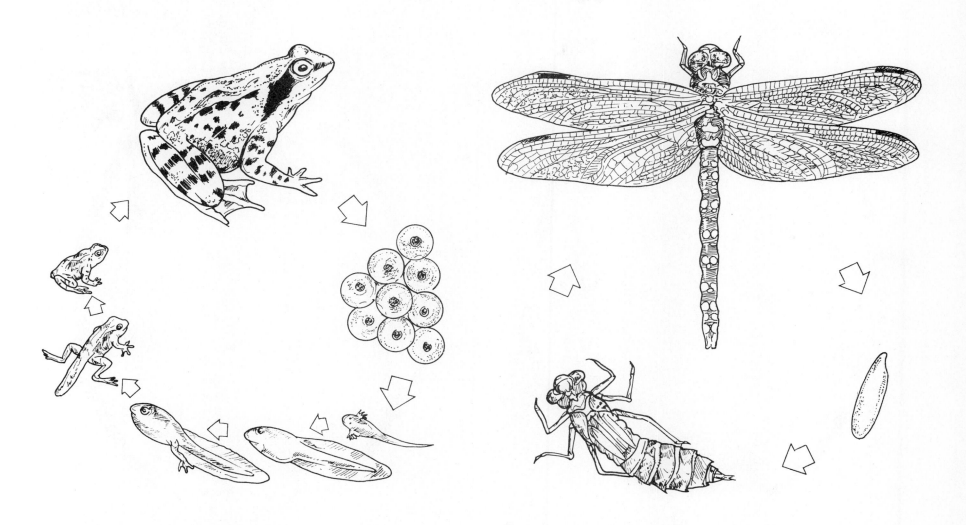

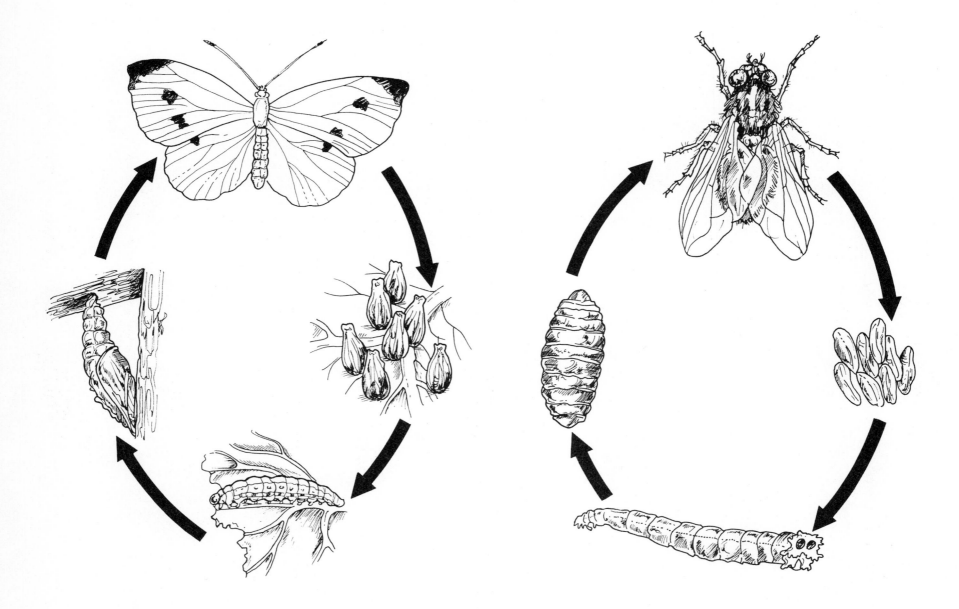

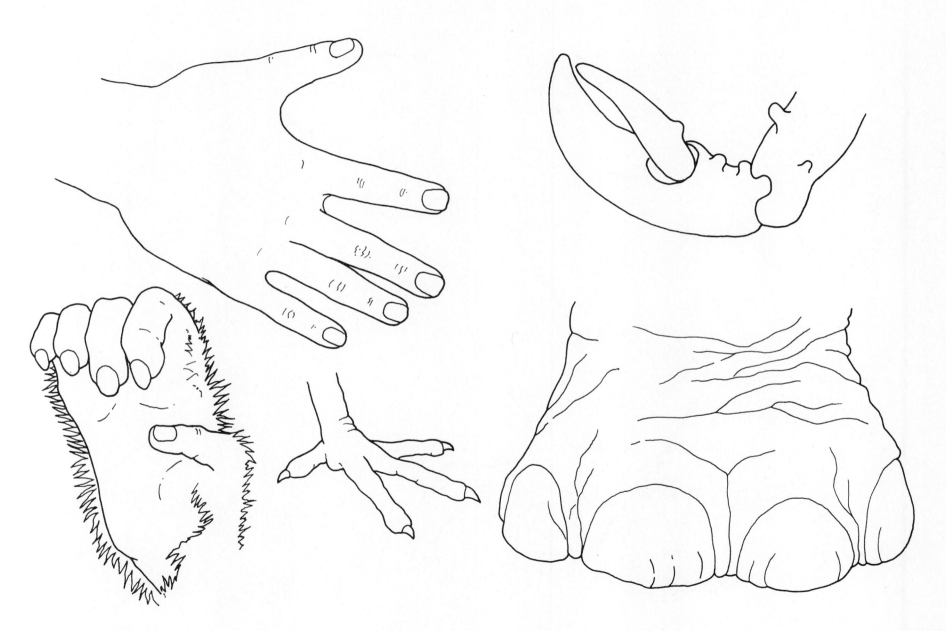

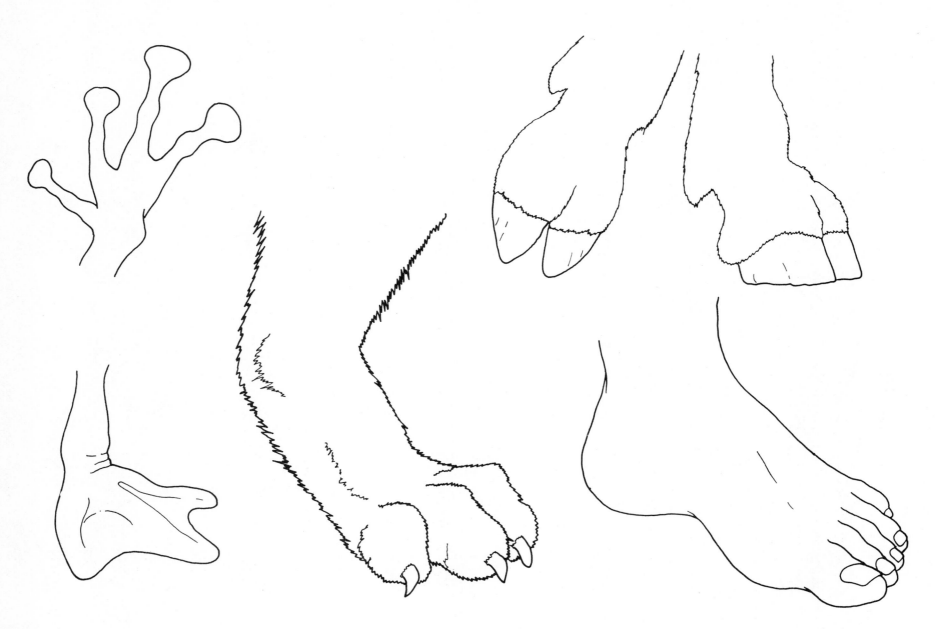

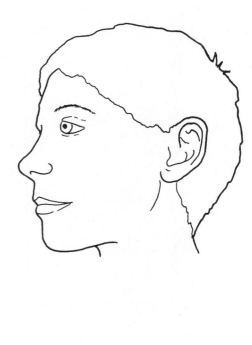

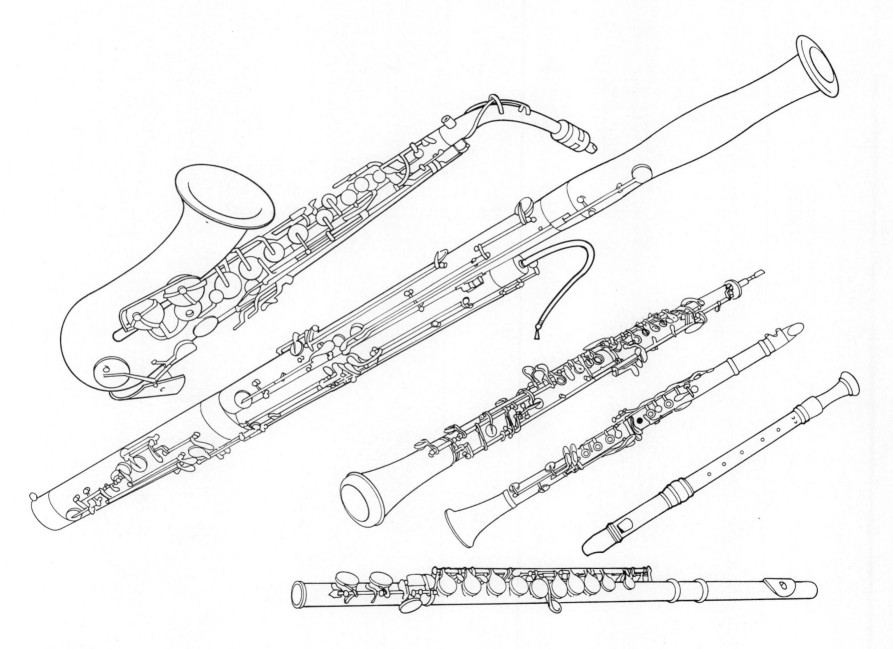

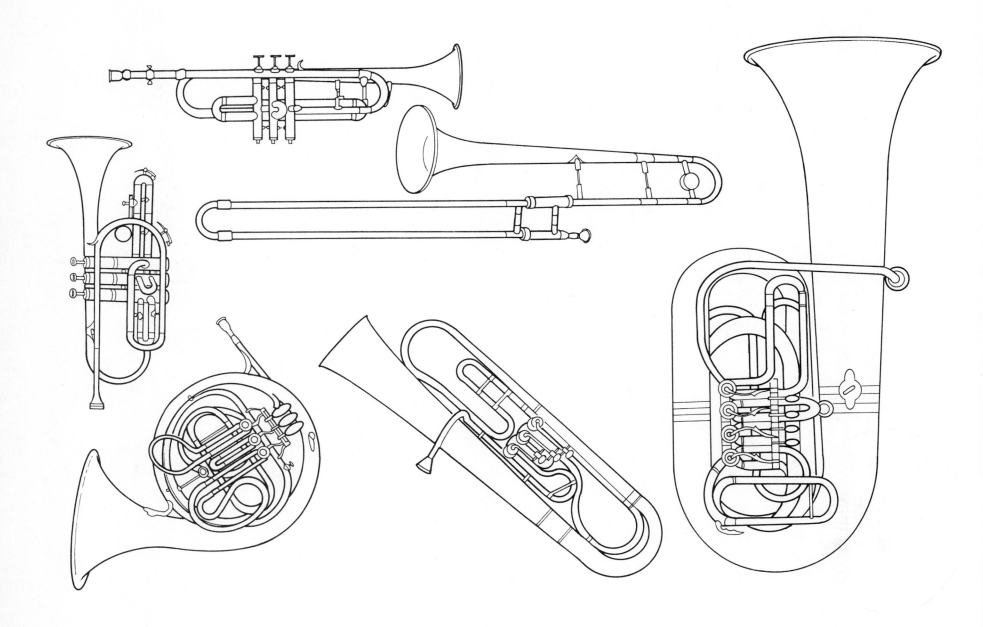

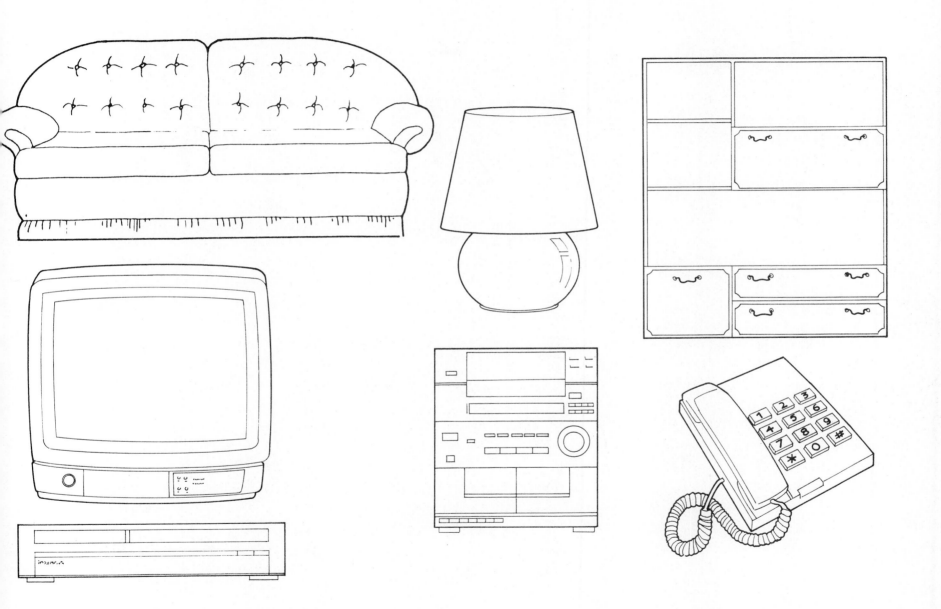

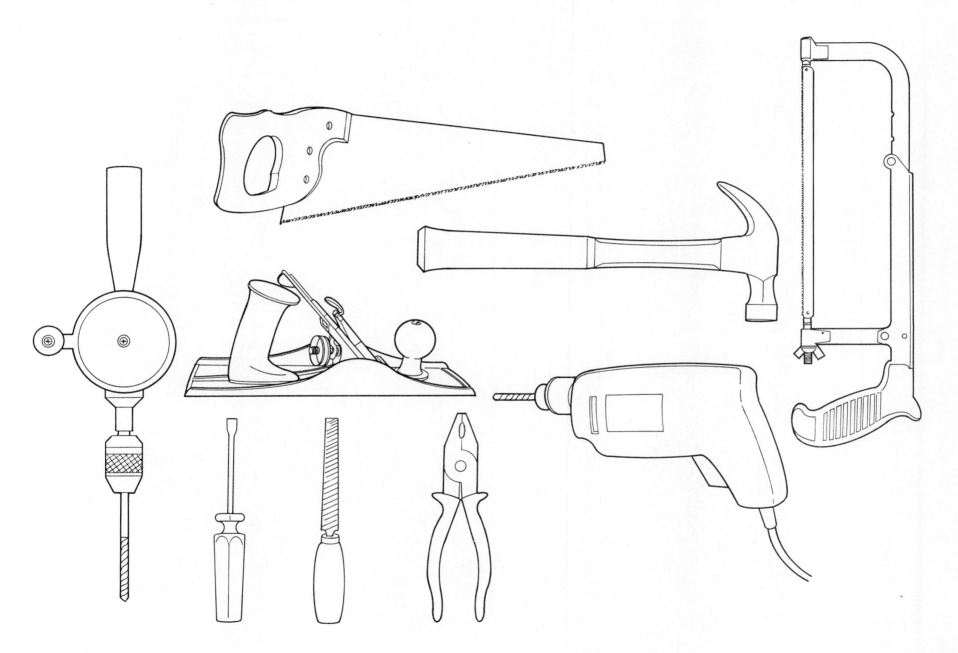

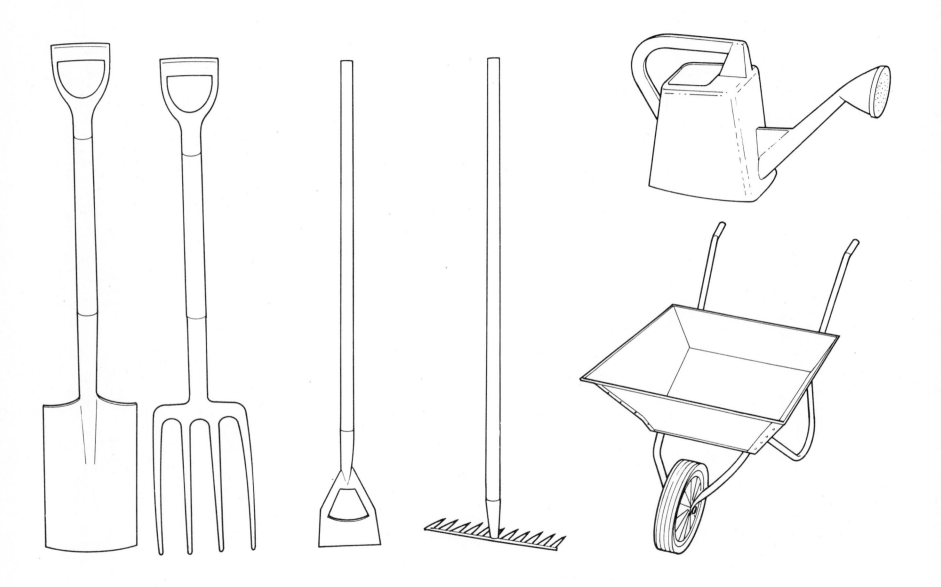

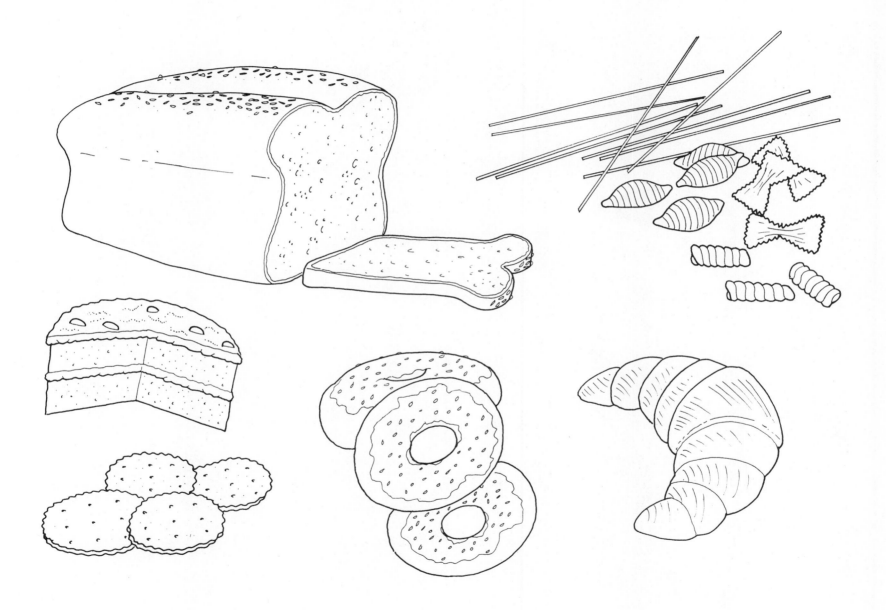

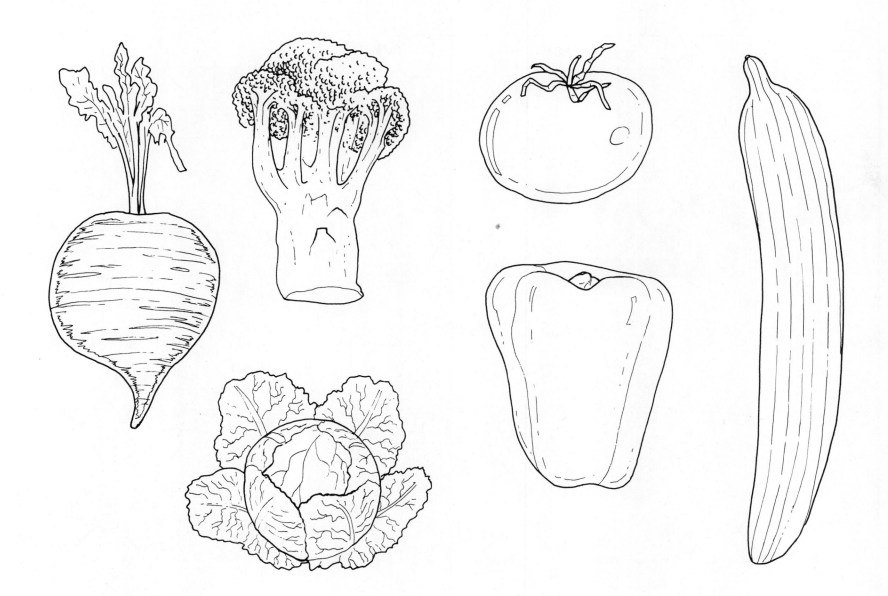

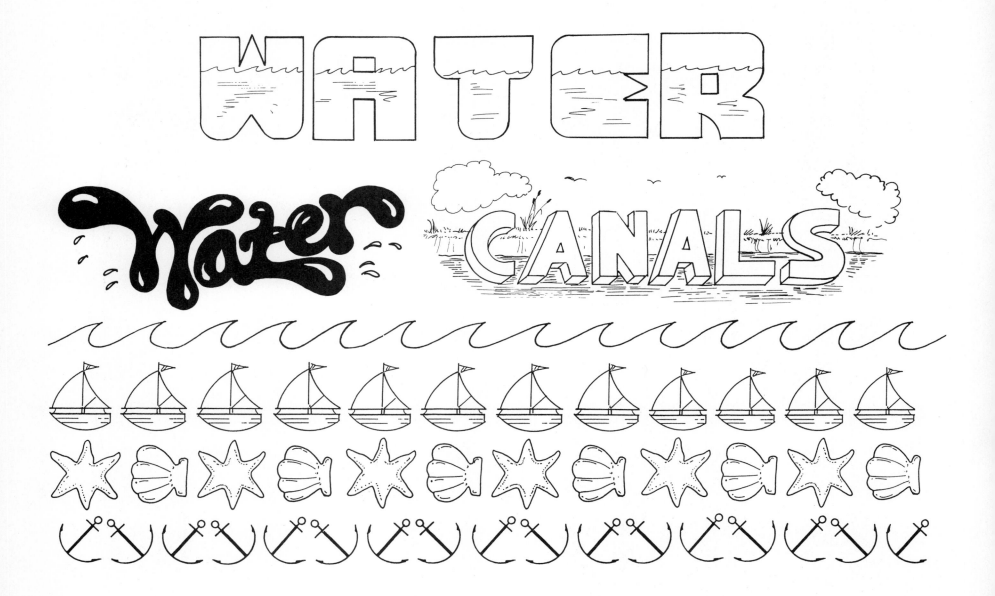

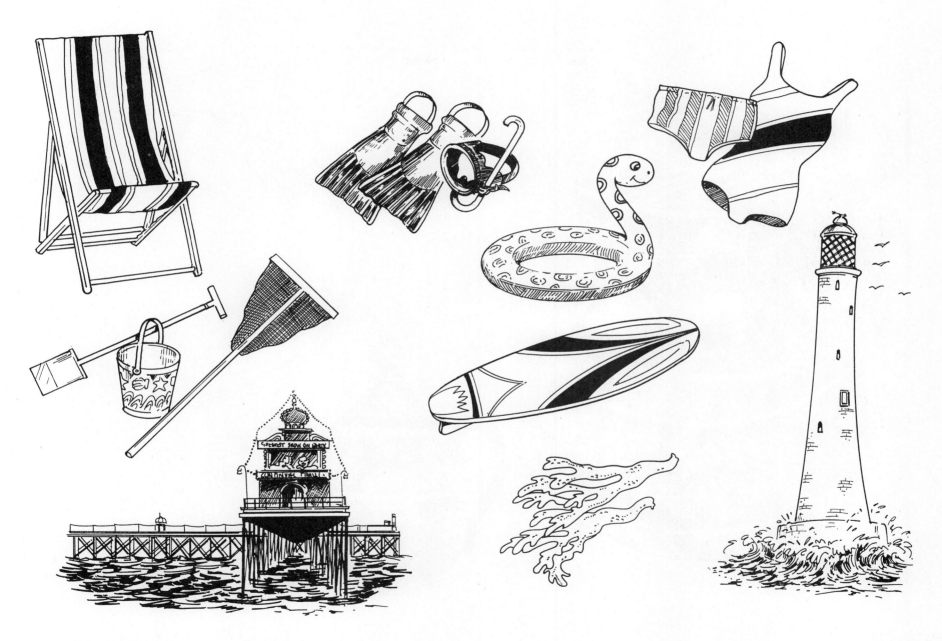

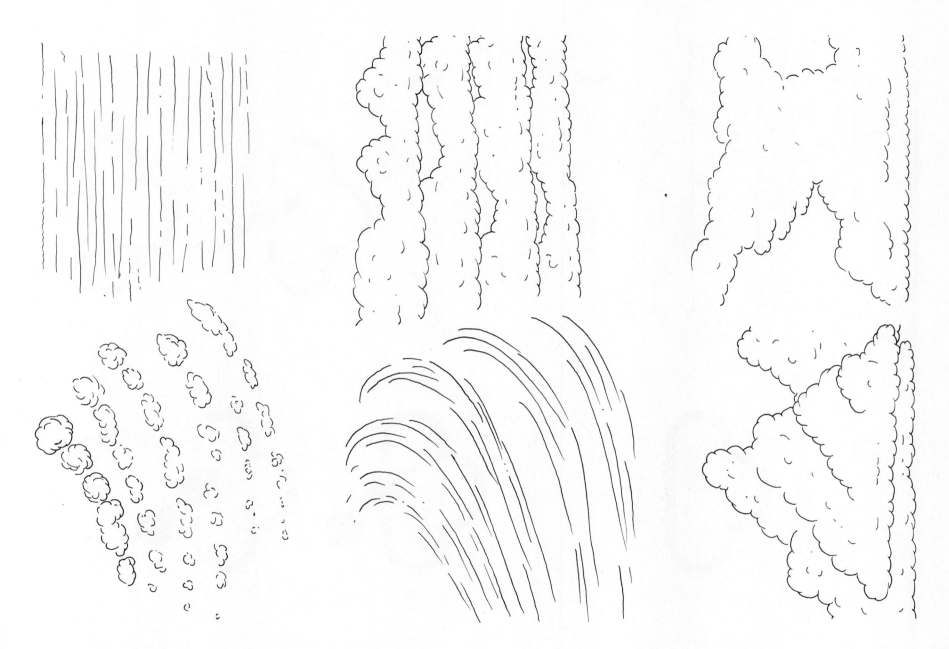

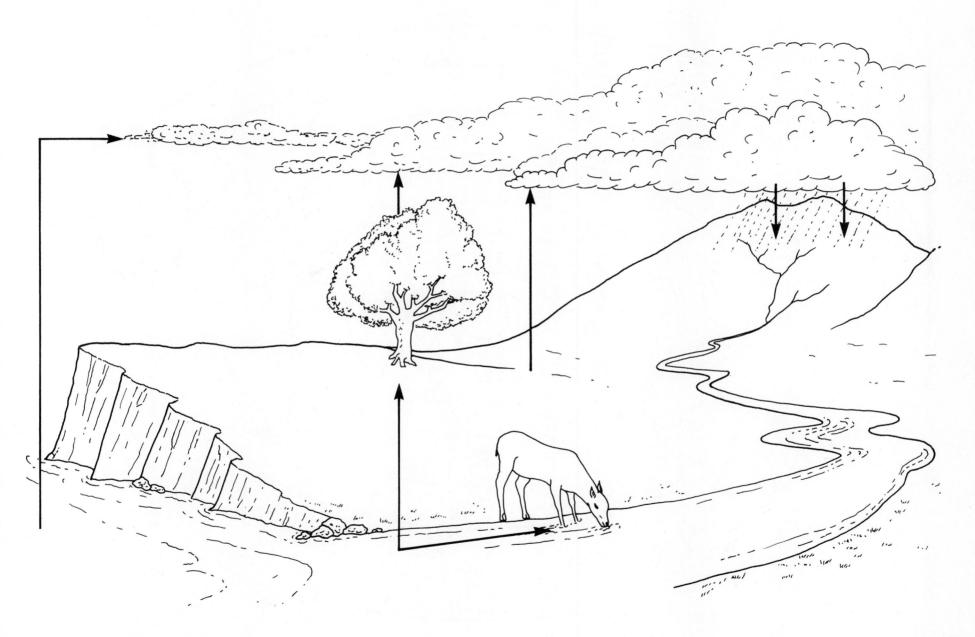

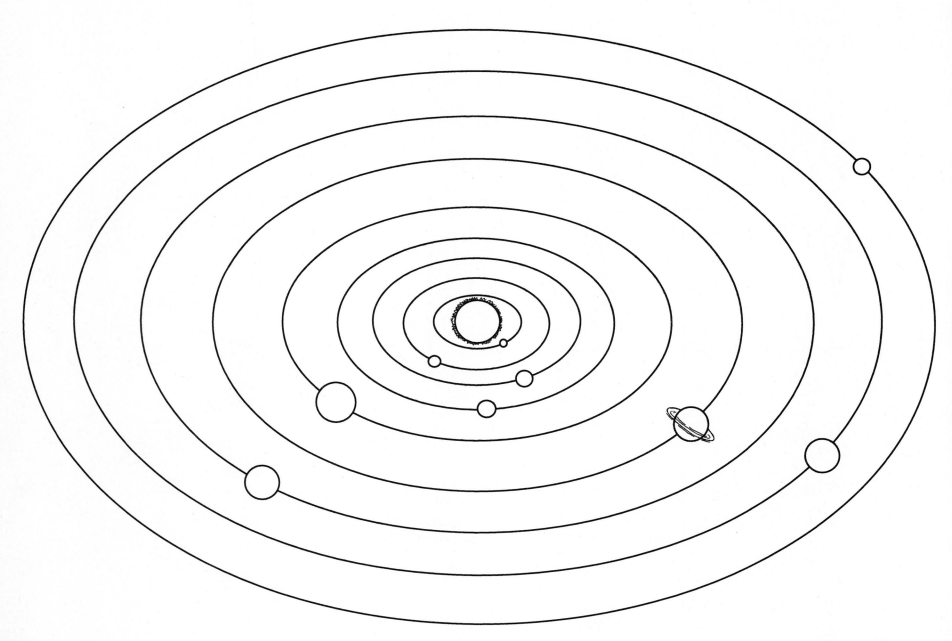

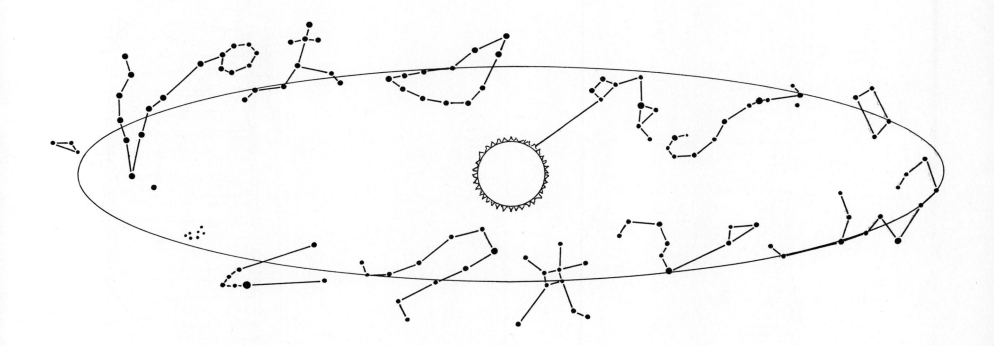

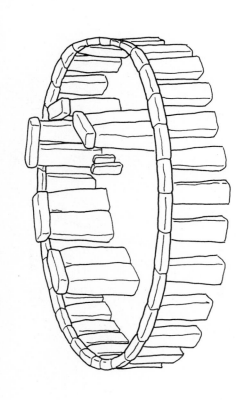

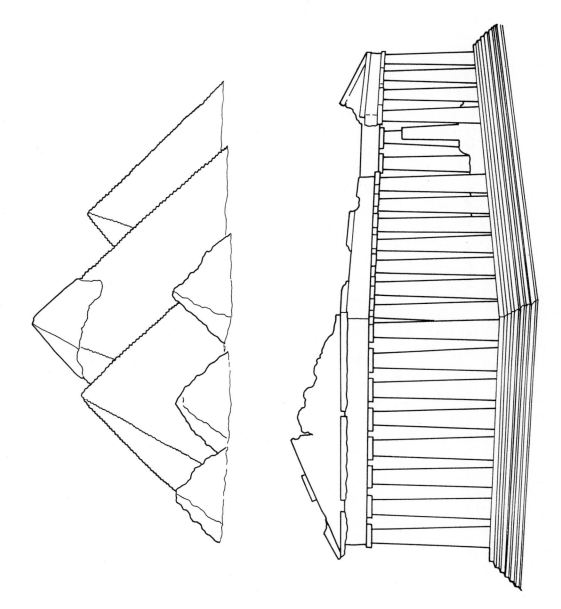

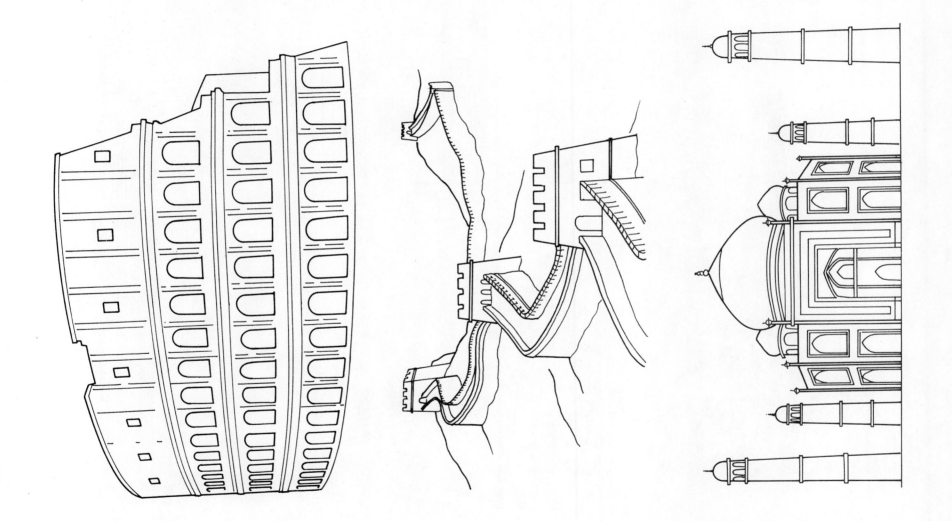

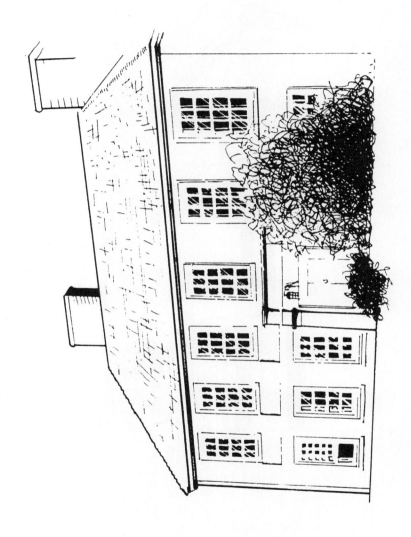

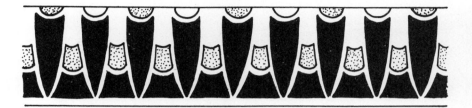

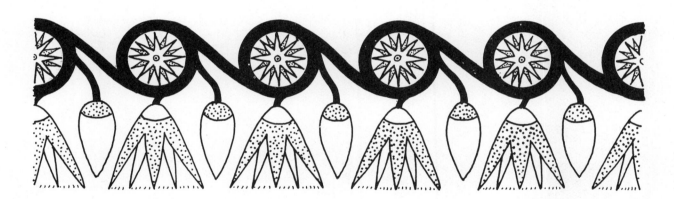

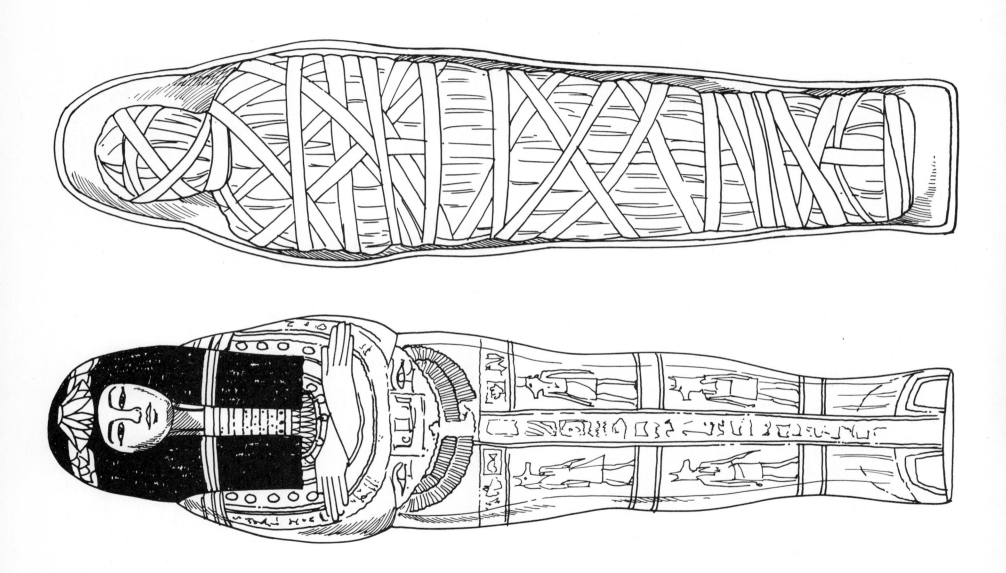

Teacher Timesavers: Art file

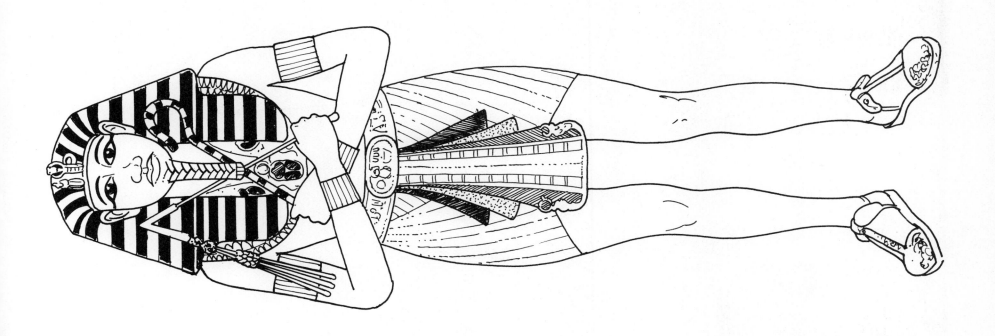

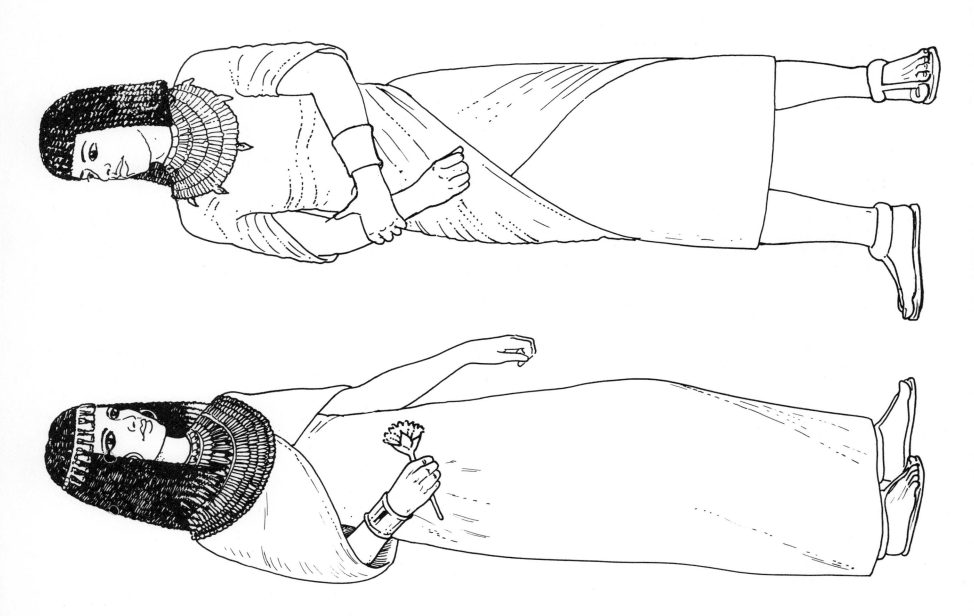

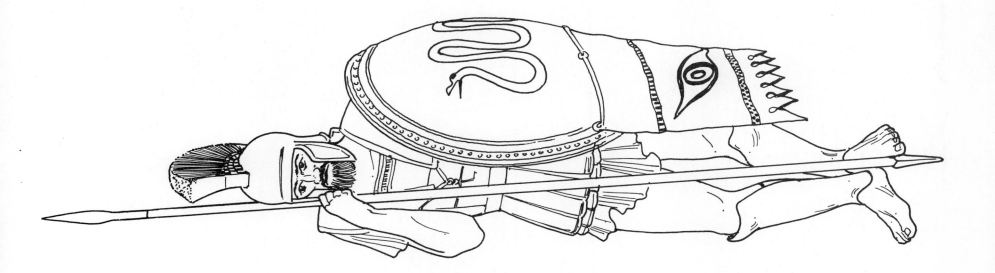

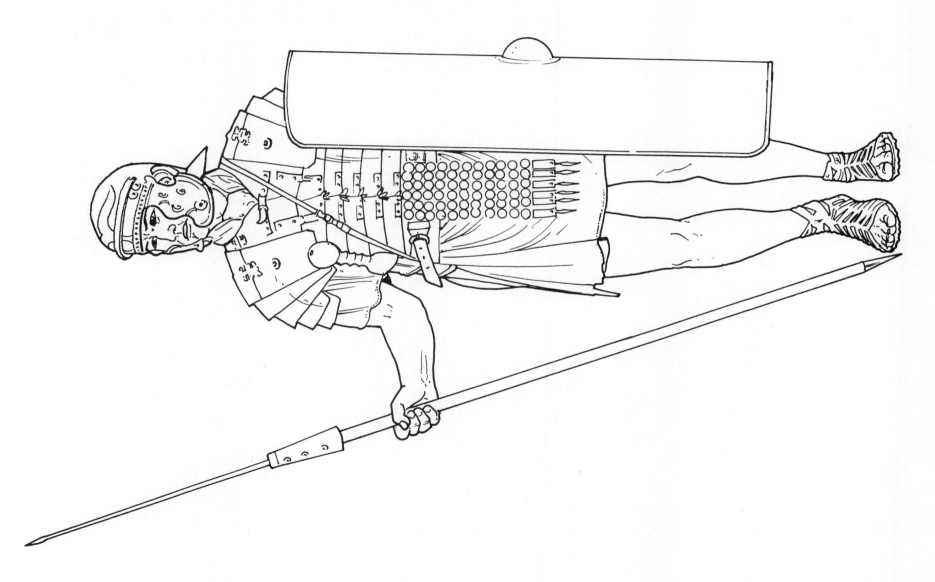

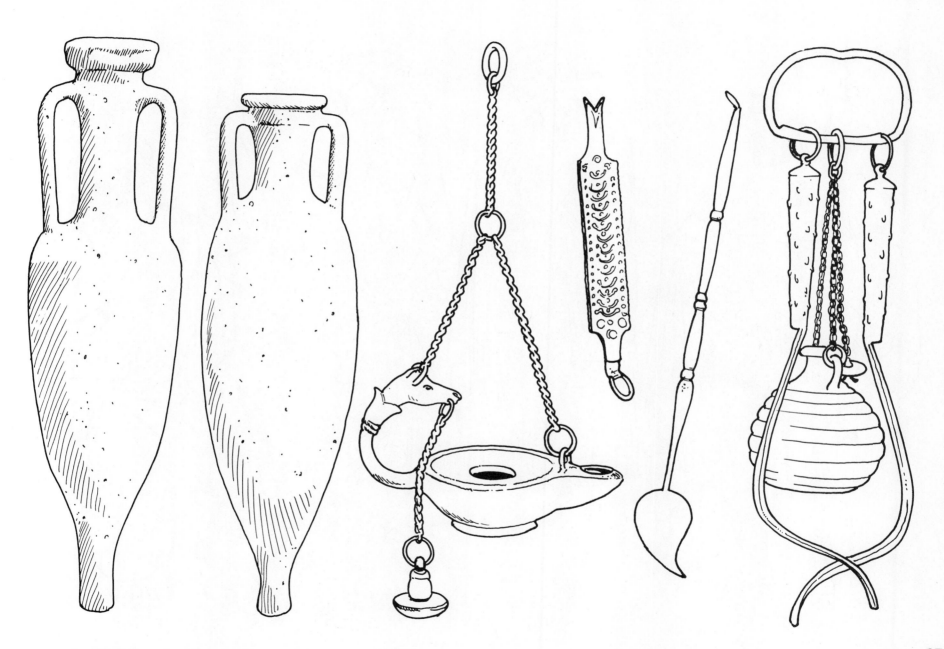

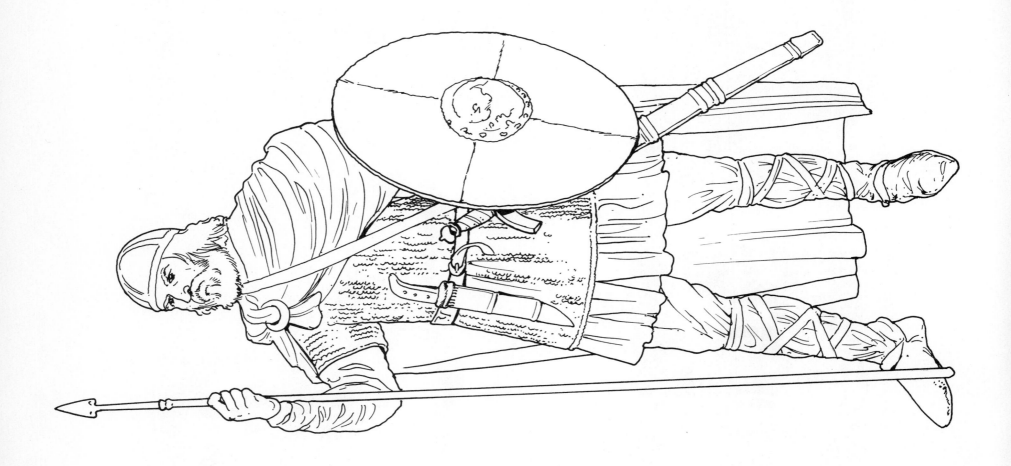

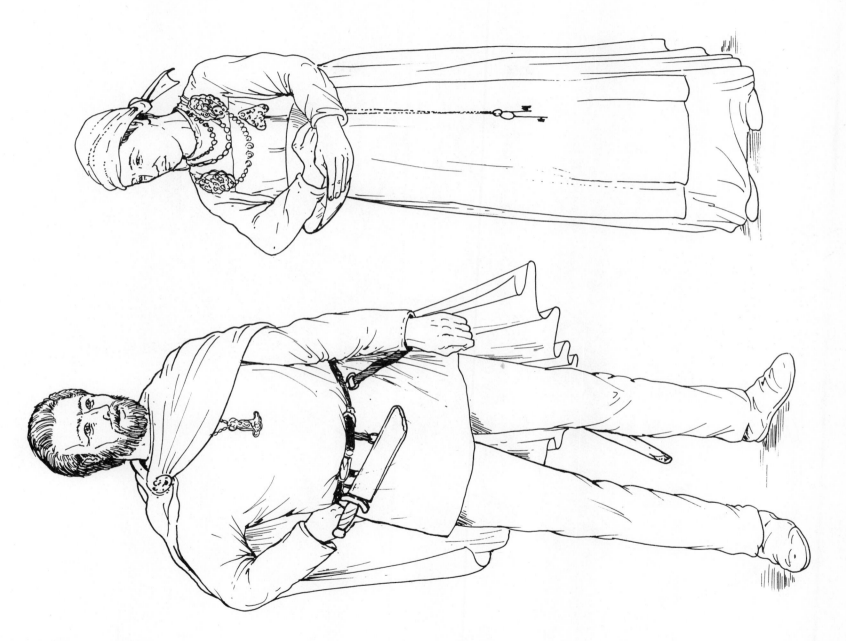

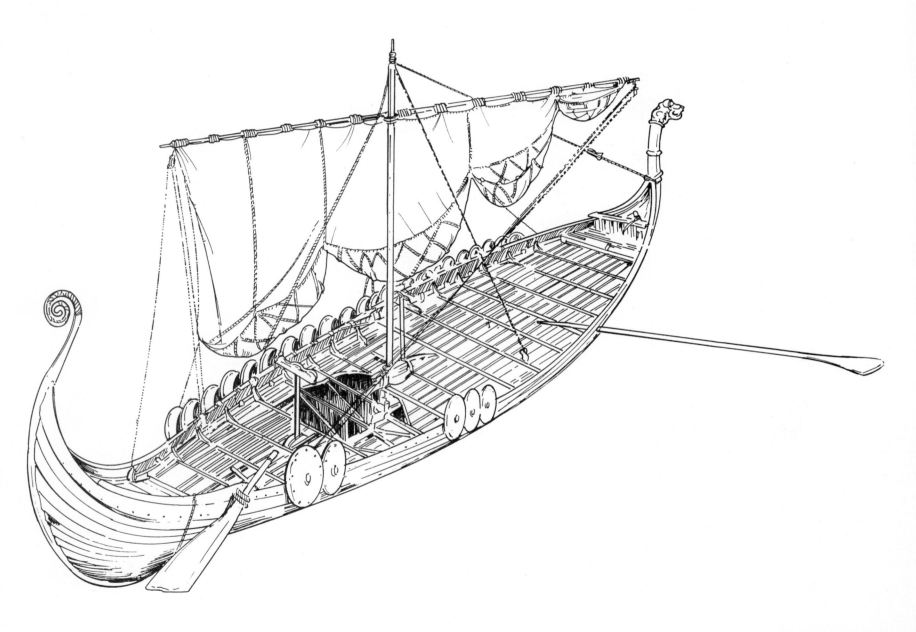

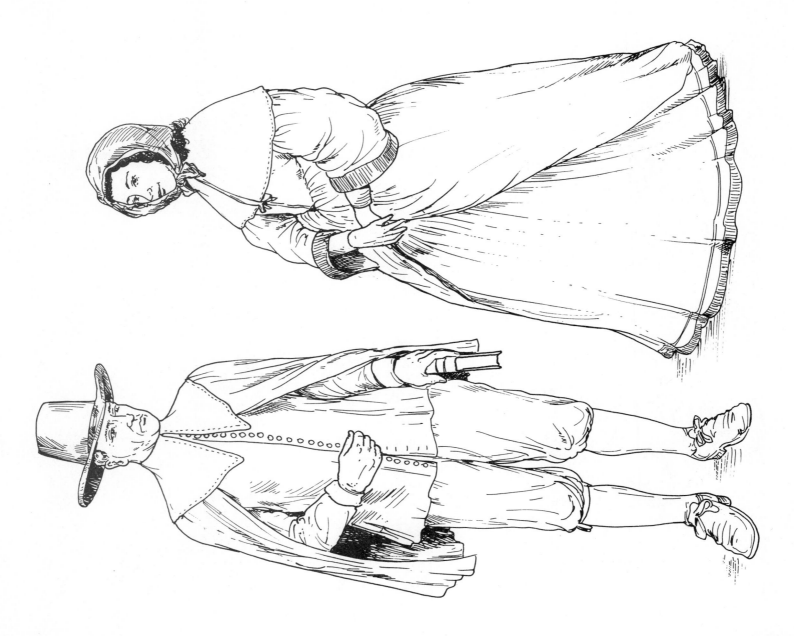

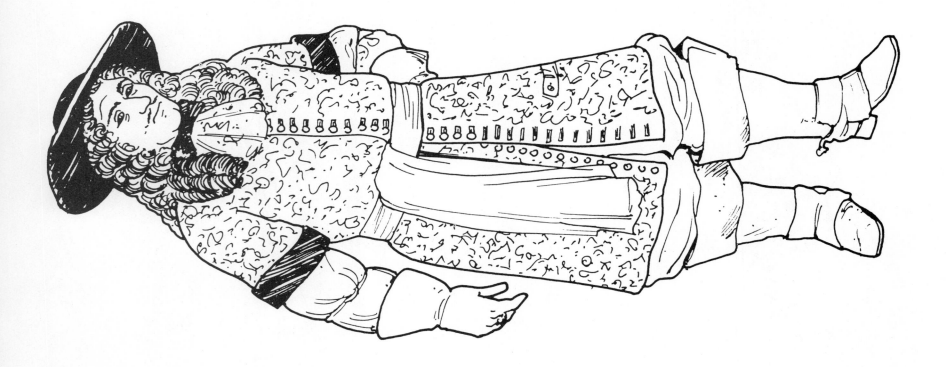

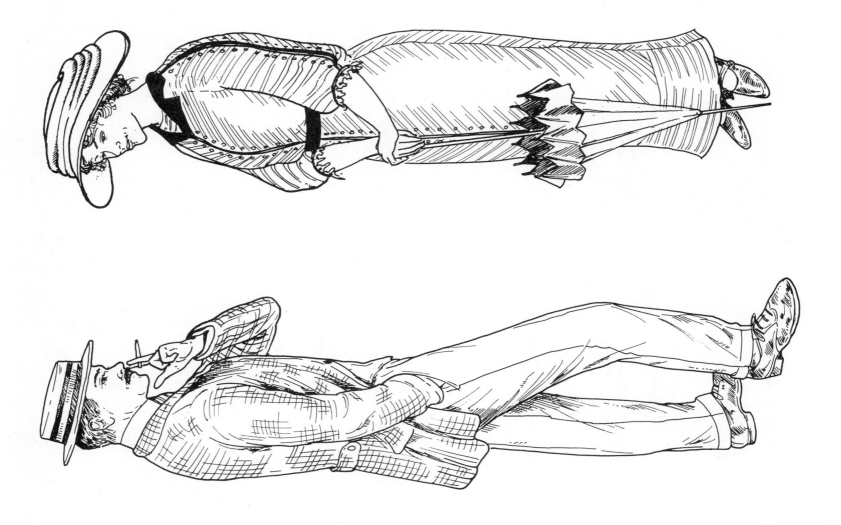

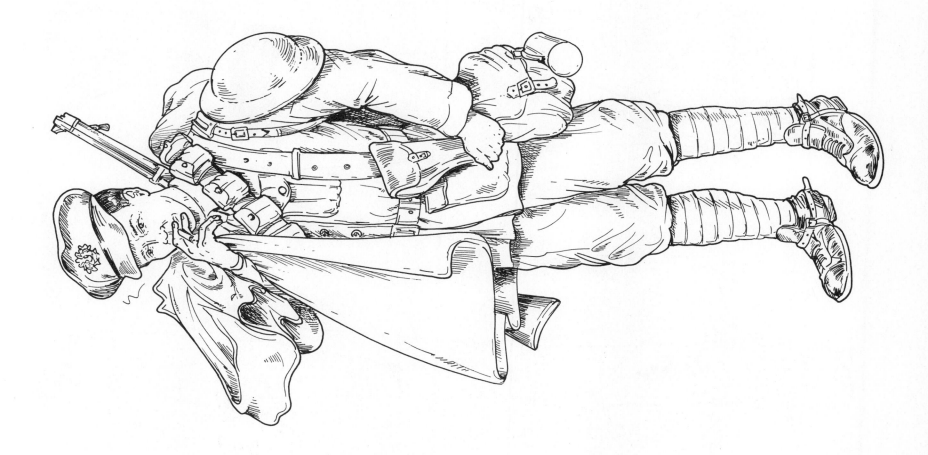

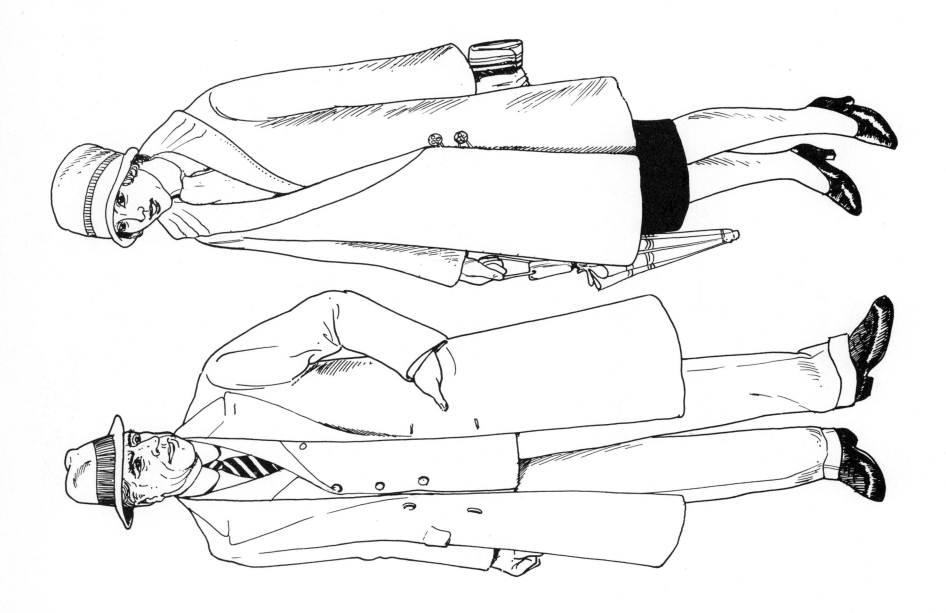

Teacher Timesavers: Art file

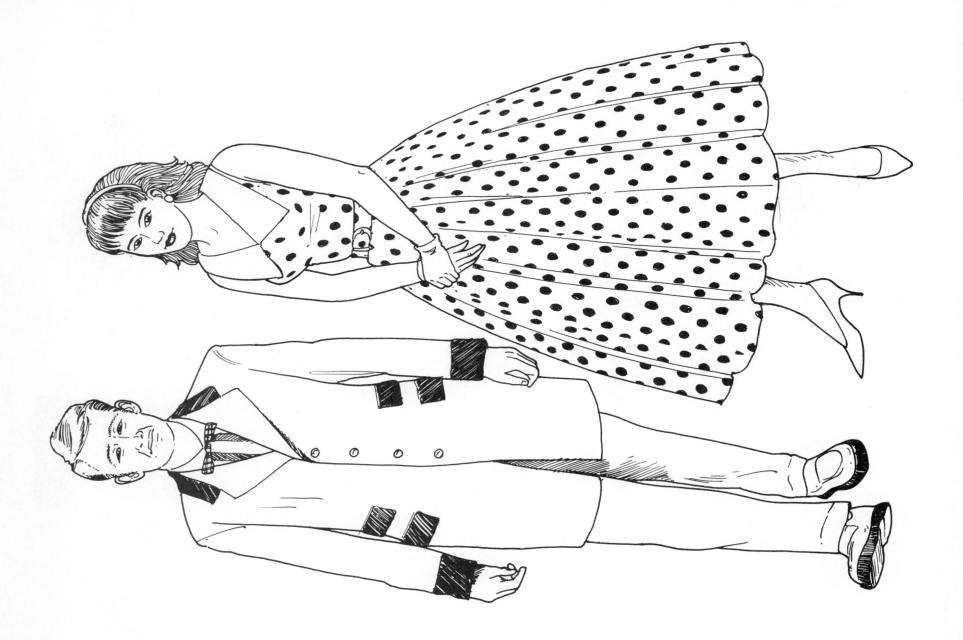

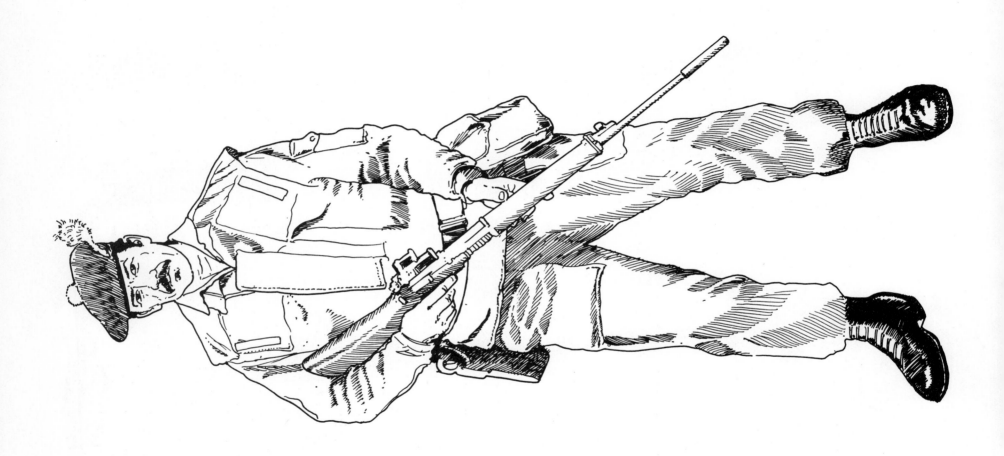

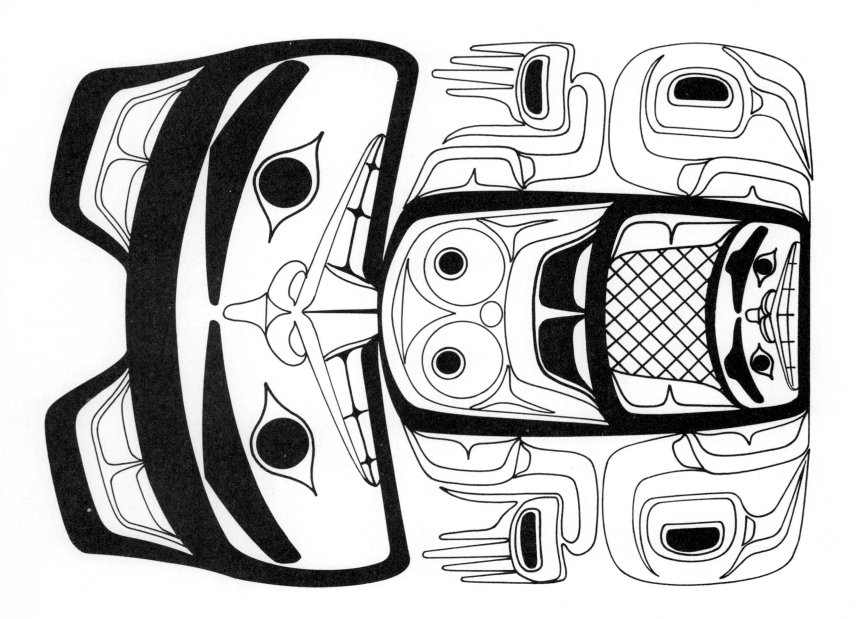

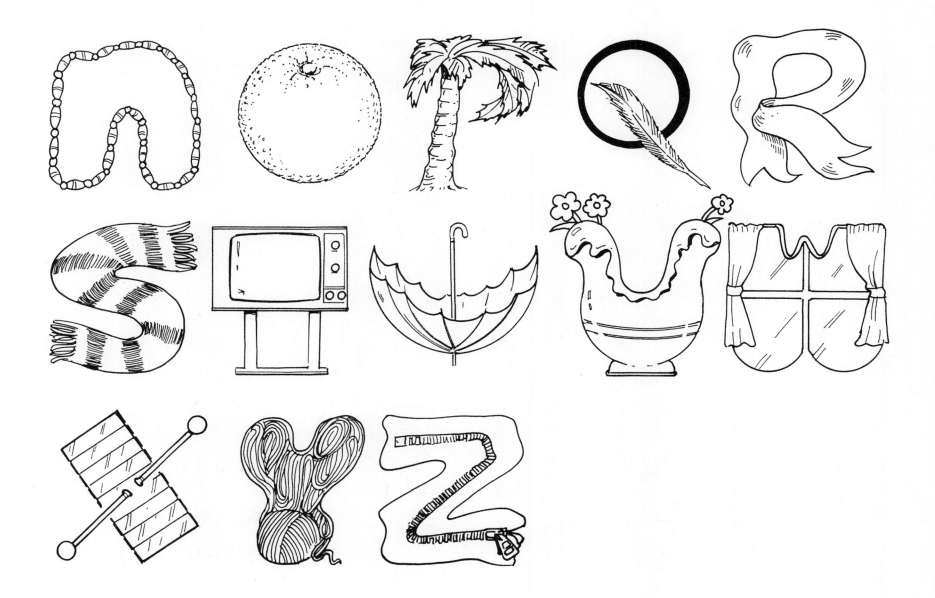

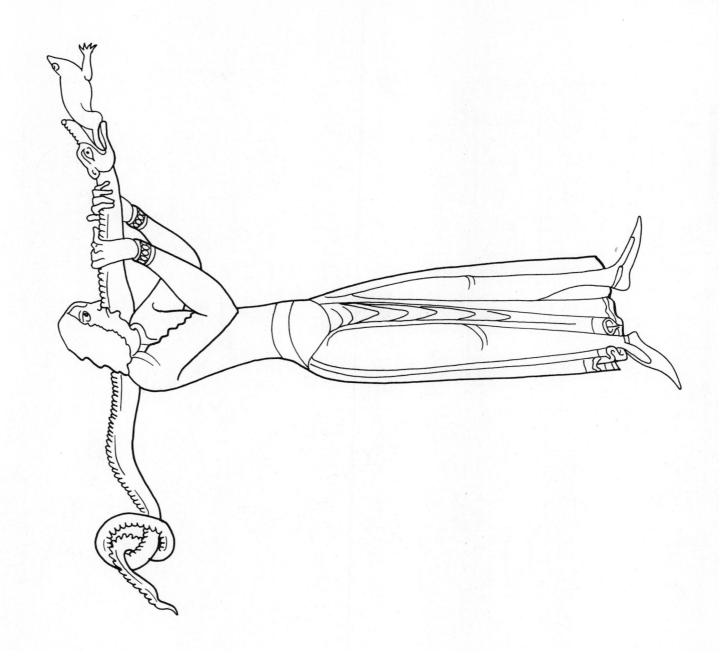

BOOKS

Pets

OUR WORLD

Pollution

Art

WELCOME

Christmas

Happy Diwali

Happy Birthday

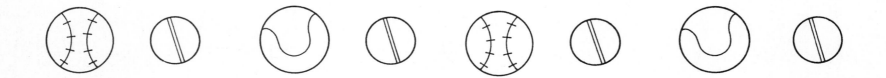

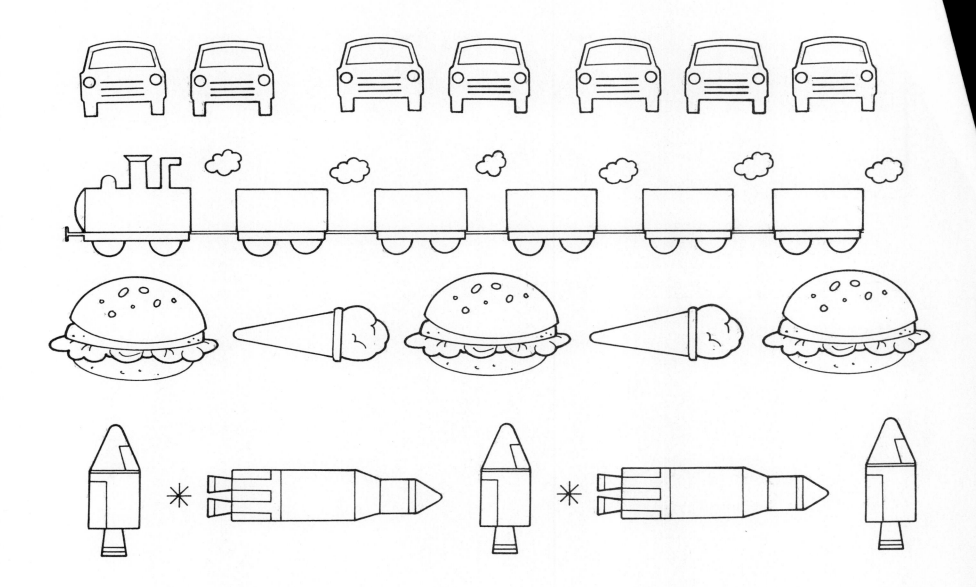

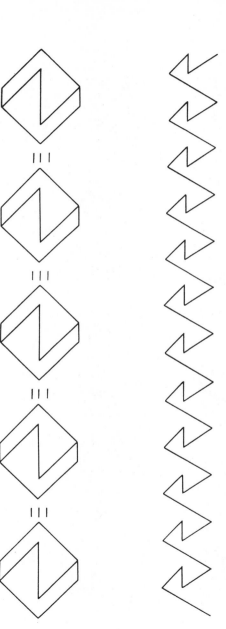

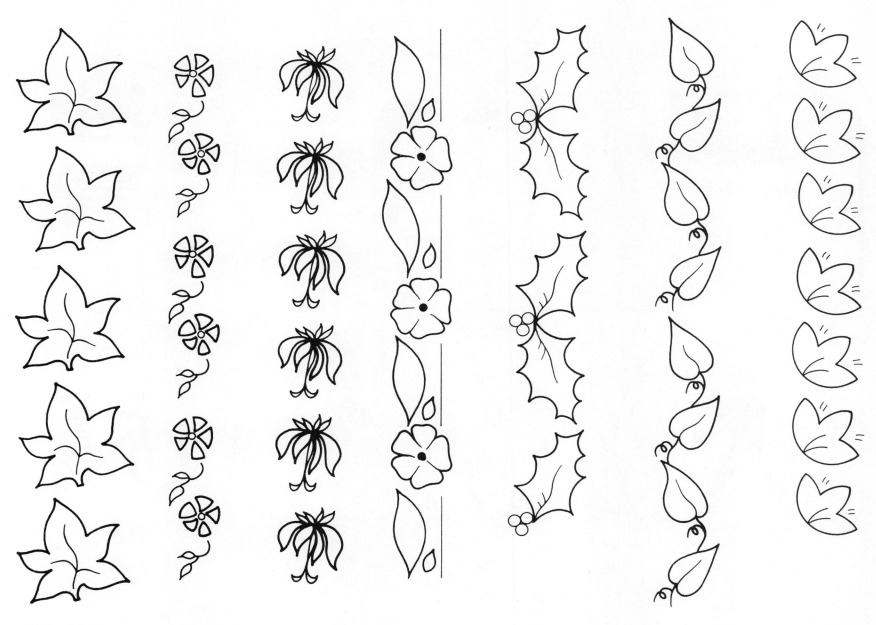

Teacher Timesavers: Art file